FIGHTING TO SURVIVE SPACE DISASTERS

TERRIFYING TRUE STORIES

By Elizabeth Raum

COMPASS POINT BOOKS
a capstone imprint

Compass Point Books are published by Capstone Press
1710 Roe Crest Drive, North Mankato, Minnesota 56003
www.capstonepub.com

Library of Congress Cataloging-in-Publication Data
Names: Raum, Elizabeth, author.
Title: Fighting to survive space disasters : terrifying true stories / by Elizabeth Raum.
Description: North Mankato, Minnesota : Capstone Press, [2019] | Series: Compass Point
books. Fighting to survive | Audience: Ages 10-14.
Identifiers: LCCN 2019005973| ISBN 9780756561864 (hardcover) | ISBN 9780756562335
(pbk.) | ISBN 978-0-7565-6208-3 (eBook PDF)
Subjects: LCSH: Space vehicle accidents—History—Juvenile literature. | Astronautics—
Accidents—History—Juvenile literature. | Survival—Juvenile literature.
Classification: LCC TL867 .R38 2019 | DDC 629.45009—dc23
LC record available at https://lccn.loc.gov/2019005973

Editorial Credits
Kristen Mohn, editor; Terri Poburka, designer; Morgan Walters, media researcher; Kathy
McColley, production specialist

Photo Credits
Alamy: TCD/Prod.DB, 17; Getty Images: Bettmann, 12, Science Source, 45, Sovfoto,
20, SVF2, 48; Granger: ITAR-TASS Photo Agency, 14; iStockphoto: peepo, (astronaut)
Cover; NASA, 6, 7, 9, 10, 24, 25, 26, 29, 40, 42-43, 53; NASA: Eric Jones, 36; NASA: JSC,
47, 49, 54, 57, 59; NASA: Kipp Teague, 32-33, 39; NASA: Spaceflight Center Collection,
35; Newscom: Album/Fine Art Images, 4, Mediadrumimages/Nasa/University/ZUMA
Press, 31, Roscosmos/ZUMA Press, 50-51, SIPA USA/SIPA, 18, UPPA/Photoshot, 5;
Shutterstock: 4Max, (earth) Cover, Isaac Marzioli, (grunge) design element, Miloje,
(grunge) design element, Peteri, 22, xpixel, (paper) 2, 3

Printed and bound in the USA.
PA71

TABLE OF CONTENTS

INTRODUCTION

Since the beginning of time, people have been curious about outer space. Science fiction writers imagined trips into space, but it was not until the 20th century that anyone actually traveled there. On October 4, 1957, the Soviet Union launched Sputnik 1. It was the first artificial satellite. The first U.S. satellite, Explorer 1, launched on January 31, 1958. The race to space had begun.

Soviet cosmonaut Yuri Gagarin was the first man in space. He orbited Earth for 108 minutes on April 12, 1961. Less than a month later, NASA sent American Alan Shepard into space. His 15-minute flight in Freedom 7 marked a successful beginning for the U.S. manned space program.

Artist's rendering of Soviet cosmonaut Yuri Gagarin, the first man in space

DANGEROUS JOURNEY

Space travelers faced dangers from the moment they began training for spaceflight. Fires, equipment malfunctions, heat shield failures, and spacesuit failures could be deadly. Since the 1960s, 31 astronauts have died while preparing for flights or on the way to space. Even those on the ground who help prepare for missions are at risk. During a 1960 Soviet launchpad disaster, 160 people on the ground were killed.

Those who accept the risks of space travel know they will be far from help and far from home. Space travel requires knowledge of the spacecraft and its operating systems. It also requires confidence in the people who design and build the ships, spacesuits, and the systems that support them. Perhaps most important of all, space travelers must be brave, quick-witted, and creative.

Alan Shepard became the second man, and first American, in space on May 5, 1961.

SPLASHDOWN!
A STORY OF LIBERTY BELL

Virgil "Gus" Grissom was the United States' second man in space. His flight, like Alan Shepard's, was suborbital. It took him 118 miles (190 kilometers) above Earth. It was designed to prove that Shepard's flight wasn't a fluke—that a person could survive spaceflight.

Grissom's launch went smoothly. So did his 15 minutes of flight. It was on his return to Earth that Gus Grissom nearly died.

Before becoming one of the country's first astronauts in 1959, Grissom had been an Air Force pilot. He was one of the seven astronauts chosen for the Mercury program, which was the first spaceflight program in U.S. history. He spent two years planning and preparing to go into space. He worked closely with the engineers who designed and built his spacecraft. He named it Liberty Bell 7 because it looked like the original Liberty Bell in Philadelphia. He chose the "7" to honor the seven astronauts in the Mercury program.

Astronaut John Glenn (right) helps Gus Grissom into the Liberty Bell 7.

Liberty Bell 7 was a small ship with just enough room for Grissom. It had a bigger viewing window than Freedom 7, Alan Shepard's space capsule. Engineers also added explosive bolts to make the hatch easier to open when the astronaut landed. NASA performed several safety checks. Although Grissom tried to be patient, he was eager for his first spaceflight.

LAUNCH

NASA scheduled the launch for July 18, 1961, but canceled due to bad weather. It was rescheduled for the next day. Again, bad weather caused a delay. Finally, in the early morning

Liberty Bell 7 lifted off on July 21, 1961, carrying Gus Grissom.

hours of July 21, 1961, Gus Grissom climbed into his space capsule. Liberty Bell 7 sailed into space at 7:20 a.m. "Liftoff was very smooth," Grissom wrote later. "I felt the booster start to vibrate and I could hear the engines start. I could feel a low vibration . . . "

He traveled through a layer of cirrus clouds and then broke through the clouds and into the blue sky. As he climbed higher, the atmosphere got darker until it "seemed jet black." The new, larger window provided a spectacular view.

REENTRY

All too soon, it was time to return to Earth.

Grissom was in control of the spacecraft. He maintained the proper altitude and fired the retrorockets, which slowed the spacecraft for landing. He felt as if he were moving backward, but that was normal. Everything seemed to be working properly.

The main parachute and the drogue chute, designed to slow the spacecraft's descent, popped out on schedule. Grissom felt a slight shock as the chutes pulled on the capsule. It bounced a bit. No problem.

Fifteen minutes and 37 seconds after liftoff, Liberty Bell 7 splashed into the Atlantic Ocean, right on schedule.

A STRANGE GURGLE

Water covered the spacecraft window, and Grissom heard a strange gurgling noise. He checked to see if any water had leaked inside the capsule. He couldn't see any. After 20 or 30 seconds, the capsule bobbed up, and the window was above water.

Following procedures, Grissom opened up the faceplate, disconnected the oxygen hose, and unfastened the helmet from his suit. Then he released the safety straps and medical sensors.

Helicopters were standing by to recover the Liberty Bell 7 and take Grissom to a waiting Navy ship. He radioed the waiting helicopter and told the pilot that he'd need a few more minutes to work the switches on the instrument panel. Once that was done, he would signal the helicopter to hook onto the capsule and lift it out of the water. Then he would remove his helmet, blow the hatch, and step onto the sill of the capsule and into a rescue sling lowered from the copter. The helicopter would pull him to safety, and he'd never have to touch the ocean.

Except . . . the hatch blew before Grissom touched it.

"All I could see was blue sky and sea water rushing in over the sill. I made just two moves, both of them instinctive. I tossed off my helmet, grabbed the right edge of the instrument panel and hoisted myself right through the hatch. I have never moved faster in my life."

Grissom checked his flight plan in preparation for his solo mission.

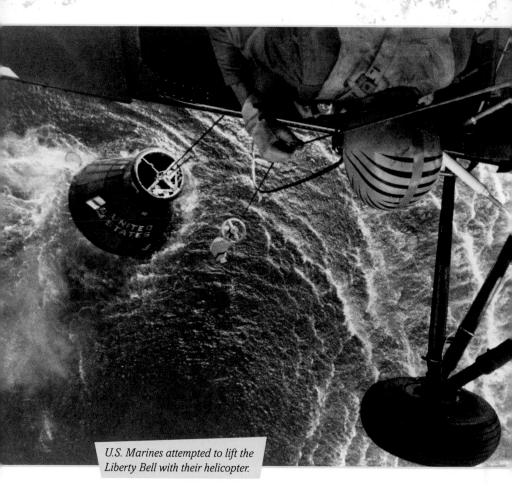

U.S. Marines attempted to lift the
Liberty Bell with their helicopter.

TOSSED INTO THE OCEAN

Grissom landed in the ocean. He became tangled in one of the
lines from the capsule, and, after a moment's panic, freed himself.
When he looked back at Liberty Bell 7, he realized that the capsule
was sinking, and he was floating in the ocean.

Fortunately, he had rolled up the rubber neck dam on his collar
so that it was tight around the neck. Although it was designed to
keep air inside the spacesuit after the astronaut took off his helmet,
it would also keep the water out of it. Grissom later said, "This was
the best thing I did all day."

RECOVERY?

A helicopter named Hunt Club 1 hovered overhead. The copilot stood in the open doorway trying to hook the cable onto Liberty Bell 7. Grissom swam closer to the capsule to help, but before he reached it, the copilot snagged the capsule with his hook. As the chopper struggled to pull the waterlogged capsule out of the water, a red warning light flashed on the helicopter's instrument panel. If the copter kept lifting the heavy capsule, the copter's engine would probably burn out. Reluctantly, the pilot cut the capsule loose.

Grissom watched the Liberty Bell 7 sink into the ocean. He had never lost a plane during his years as a pilot. Now, on his first spaceflight, he'd failed to bring Liberty Bell 7 home. He'd had no choice, but still, he felt upset even as he struggled for his own survival.

Grissom's spacesuit weighed 22 pounds (10 kilograms) when dry. As souvenirs for his sons and their friends, he'd carried into space two rolls of 50 dimes. They were still in his spacesuit. Air inside the suit was supposed to help an astronaut float, but the air was escaping through a hole in the suit. Not only was air leaking out through the hole—water was flowing in. Without the air to keep it afloat, Grissom had to fight to keep the heavy suit from pulling him underwater.

DID YOU KNOW?

The Liberty Bell 7 had a white, irregular paint stripe on it starting at the base and extending up toward the top. It was made to look like the crack in the Liberty Bell in Philadelphia.

SINKING

Grissom was sinking as surely as the Liberty Bell 7 had sunk. He glanced around. Were there sharks nearby? He suspected there were. He swallowed water as the waves washed over him. Would anyone come to his rescue? He waved his arms, and the men in the copters waved back, not seeming to register his distress. "I wasn't scared now," he wrote later. "I was angry."

But pilots Jim Lewis and John Reinhard, on Hunt Club 1, didn't realize that Grissom was in trouble. Neither did other nearby helicopters. Their rotor blades kicked up the water. Giant waves washed over Grissom's head. "I had to swim hard just to keep my head up," he said later.

Grissom was lifted from the ocean as the Liberty Bell 7 sank in the Atlantic Ocean.

Finally, a helicopter approached, dragging a rescue collar. Grissom grabbed the collar and tossed it over his neck and under his arms. It was on backward, but that didn't matter. It kept him afloat. The copter dragged him about 15 feet (4.6 meters) before it was able to pull him up and inside to safety. Grissom was exhausted by the time he was delivered to the Navy carrier. He slipped a life jacket over his spacesuit, not wanting to risk another chance of drowning.

THE LOST LIBERTY BELL

There was no chance of recovering the Liberty Bell 7 at the time. It fell 3 miles (4.8 km) beneath the ocean surface. Grissom was sorry to lose his ship, but it wasn't his fault. NASA investigated the incident. Although some people blamed Grissom, NASA officials did not. He flew again in March 1965 as part of the Gemini program.

Sadly, in 1967 Grissom and two other astronauts died during a prelaunch test for the Apollo 1 mission. Fully understanding the dangers of his career, Grissom said two years before his death, "The conquest of space is worth the risk of life."

DID YOU KNOW?

In 1999 a team supported by the Discovery Channel recovered the Liberty Bell 7 from the bottom of the ocean. It's now on display at the Kansas Cosmosphere & Space Center. Why the hatch blew open is still a mystery.

CAUGHT OUTSIDE!
A STORY OF VOSKHOD

Cosmonaut Alexei Leonov of the Soviet Union took the world's first spacewalk. He and fellow cosmonaut Pavel Belyayev made up a two-man crew. Soviet newspapers reported the walk in glowing terms. They considered it a success because both cosmonauts survived. However, the real story remained secret for years. We now know that Leonov nearly died during his spacewalk, and both he and Belyayev faced several more dangers before and after their return to Earth.

Cosmonaut Alexei Leonov, 1965

SPACEWALK

On the morning of March 18, 1965, Leonov and Belyayev climbed into the Voskhod-2, ready for blastoff. Both men wore bulky spacesuits. The launch went perfectly, and Voskhod-2 began orbiting Earth. The cosmonauts did a routine check. Their goal was to set speed and altitude records while completing the spacewalk.

Everything seemed fine, so Belyayev inflated the airlock that Leonov would use to exit the spacecraft. Leonov strapped on his life-support system and crawled into the airlock. He closed the connecting hatch behind him and waited there while Belyayev adjusted the air pressure inside the airlock. Because there is zero pressure in space, adjusting the air pressure would protect Leonov against decompression sickness.

When Belyayev gave him the "go" signal, Leonov opened the hatch and floated into space. A tether connected him to Voskhod-2. He mounted a camera on the airlock to take photos of the spacewalk. When Leonov looked down, he saw Earth far beneath his feet. He later said he felt "like a seagull with its wings outstretched, soaring high above the Earth."

One of Leonov's tasks was to experiment with movement outside the craft. He kicked off the side of the Voskhod-2 and went spinning into space. His tether pulled him to a stop.

DID YOU KNOW?

Spacesuits protect spacewalkers from the lack of air pressure and extreme cold outside the spacecraft. On Earth the atmosphere is about 78 percent nitrogen, 21 percent oxygen, and 1 percent other gases. Earth's atmosphere allows us to breathe. There is no air in space, so a spacesuit's life-support system provides oxygen to the astronaut, supplies the atmospheric pressure needed to survive, and protects against the cold.

TROUBLE

After 10 minutes in space, Leonov was supposed to return to the capsule. That's when he realized that his spacesuit had blown up like a balloon. It had become stiff due to the lack of atmospheric pressure. He said, "My feet had pulled away from my boots and my fingers no longer reached the gloves attached to my sleeves. . . . Now the suit was so misshapen that it would be impossible for me to enter the airlock feet first as I had in training."

He had to find a way to reduce the pressure in the spacesuit. Otherwise, he wouldn't be able to use his hands to open the airlock. He'd be stuck outside with no way inside. He knew checking with his command center on the ground would take more time than he had. He decided to open the pressure valve in the spacesuit and release oxygen a little at a time as he inched toward the airlock opening. The change in pressure caused him to feel pins and needles in his arms and legs—an early symptom of decompression sickness, which can be deadly. Releasing oxygen also meant there was less of it for him to breathe, so he had to work quickly before he lost consciousness.

Leonov felt the temperature in his suit rise dangerously high. The heat traveled from his feet up his legs and arms. His struggles to move to the airlock increased his temperature even more. He wrote, "It was taking far longer than it was supposed to. Even when I at last managed to pull myself entirely into the airlock, I had to

A 2017 Russian film, The Spacewalker, told the story of the space race and Leonov's historic spacewalk.

perform another almost impossible maneuver. I had to curl my body round in order to . . . close the airlock." Sweat dripped into his eyes, so he had to complete the task without being able to see clearly.

Once he closed the airlock, he had to wait for the pressure in the airlock to match that in the space capsule. By the time he finally made it into the capsule, perspiration soaked his body.

SPINNING

Leonov took off his helmet and wiped the sweat from his face. The Voskhod-2 was 46 seconds behind schedule. This slight delay would be enough to cause major problems at landing.

The spacewalk wasn't complete until the cosmonauts released the airlock. They fired a small explosive charge that sent it into space. But as soon as they did, the spacecraft began to spin, disorienting them. Even worse, the oxygen level inside the capsule began to climb. In a high-oxygen environment, any small spark from the engines would cause flames to erupt inside the capsule.

An external camera captured images of Leonov during his spacewalk. Audio recording of his labored breathing was later used in the movie 2001: A Space Odyssey.

The cosmonauts managed to lower the temperature, but there was little they could do to stop the spinning. Firing another rocket would require using more fuel, and they only had enough to make one course correction. They didn't dare do it. They might need that fuel to direct their landing. So, for the 22 hours until landing, they continued to spin.

A NEW PROBLEM

When the cosmonauts checked their instruments again, they discovered another problem—the automatic guidance program wasn't working. They switched it off. They would have to guide the capsule themselves. Leonov began calculating where they could land. It was a good thing they had saved that extra fuel. They would need every bit to reach the new landing spot.

The capsule was heading directly for Moscow, but they couldn't land in the middle of a big city. On the other hand, if they went too far east, they would land in China. At the time, the two countries weren't on friendly terms. Leonov chose a rural area outside the Russian city of Perm near the Ural Mountains. Landing there was less likely to cause harm.

"We can make only one attempt at reentry," Belyayev said. He asked Mission Control to go into emergency status. No other cosmonauts had ever fired the retrorockets by hand, but Leonov and Belyayev had no choice.

CRASH!

Belyayev fired the engines. "We heard them roar and felt a strong jerk as they slowed our craft," he said later. Ten seconds after that, the landing module should have separated from the orbital module. But again, something went wrong. A cable connecting the two modules failed to release. The landing module began spinning around the cable. The force of gravity increased and became so strong that it broke some small blood vessels in the cosmonauts' eyes.

Finally, the cable burned through, the spinning stopped, and the big parachutes designed to create a soft landing took over. For a few minutes, everything was peaceful.

The landing module entered the clouds. Leonov and Belyayev couldn't see anything until the spacecraft stopped. It made a gentle landing in 6 feet (1.8 m) of snow.

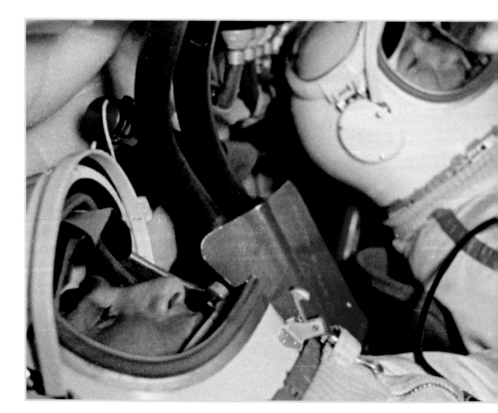

ESCAPE

The cosmonauts had landed in a dense forest 1,200 miles (1,930 km) from where they were supposed to be. They wanted to get out of the landing craft to check their surroundings, but the hatch wouldn't budge. A big birch tree blocked it.

The cosmonauts rocked back and forth until the ship moved slightly. When Belyayev pushed with all his strength, the hatch opened. The cool air felt great. Both cosmonauts inhaled deeply. At last, they were on back on Earth.

They squeezed out of the spacecraft and sank into snow up to their chins. The sky darkened and more snow began falling, so they climbed back inside and began broadcasting their location. They hoped to alert rescuers.

As they settled in to wait, they realized that the forest was home to bears and wolves. It was spring, which is mating season and a time when animals become more aggressive. The men had one pistol in the spacecraft and lots of ammunition. They might have to use it.

They heard howling, but it was just the wind.

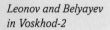

Leonov and Belyayev in Voskhod-2

FREEZING

Had anyone heard the distress signal? They learned later that a radio station in West Germany had picked it up. So did a plane flying overhead. The radio station and the plane spread the word. A search party began looking for the missing cosmonauts.

Later that afternoon, Leonov and Belyayev heard a helicopter. They struggled through the snow into a clearing and waved their arms to signal the pilot. A military helicopter would know what to

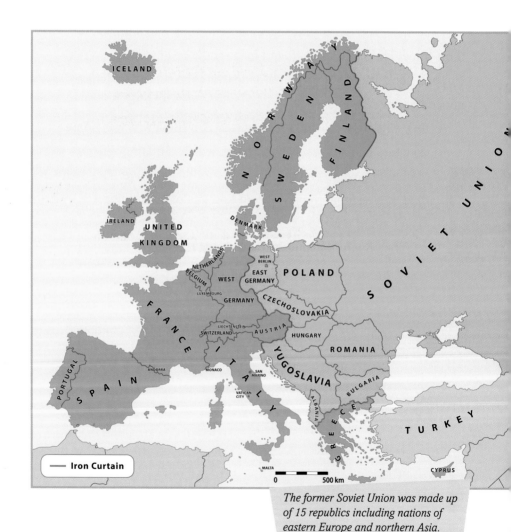

The former Soviet Union was made up of 15 republics including nations of eastern Europe and northern Asia.

do, but this one was a private copter. The pilot had no idea how to help. Even so, he tried. He tossed a rope ladder to the cosmonauts, but the bulky spacesuits that they had kept on for warmth made climbing impossible.

Other planes circled overhead. Crews tossed out warm pants, jackets, an axe, and even two pairs of wolfskin boots. Most of the items got caught in the surrounding trees, but Leonov and Belyayev were able to retrieve the boots.

Night fell. The temperature dropped. Leonov's spacesuit was sopping wet from the earlier perspiration. He was afraid he would get frostbite. Both men stripped naked, wrung out their underwear, and put it back on. They then removed the soft lining from the spacesuits and put on the linings before climbing into the space capsule. The temperature that night reached minus 13 degrees Fahrenheit (minus 25 degrees Celsius).

RESCUE

The next morning they heard voices. Leonov fired a flare. Soon a rescue team on skis, including a doctor, a cameraman, and a fellow cosmonaut, reached Leonov and Belyayev. The rescuers brought warm clothes and food. They made a delicious feast of cheese, sausage, and bread.

The rescuers built a little hut where they spent a second night. The next morning, the cosmonauts and the rescue team skied about 5.5 miles (9 km) to reach a waiting helicopter. When Leonov and Belyayev finally reached home, they were greeted as heroes. They hadn't faced just one problem, but several, and they managed to survive them all. Even more remarkable, they had completed the first spacewalk.

SPINNING!
A STORY OF GEMINI

Following the early Mercury missions, which included Gus Grissom's Liberty Bell 7, NASA developed the Gemini program. Gemini was an important step in preparing for a moon landing. Its spacecraft were designed for two astronauts, and each mission had a particular goal. For example, on June 3, 1965, Ed White became the first American to walk in space during the flight of Gemini 4. Gemini 8's mission also included a spacewalk. Astronaut David Scott performed that task. In addition, Gemini 8 would dock, or link, two spacecraft together in space for the first time. This was an important step because astronauts who landed on the moon would have to dock with the command module in order to return to Earth. NASA scientists and the astronauts planned and practiced on the ground, but the real test would occur during Gemini 8's flight.

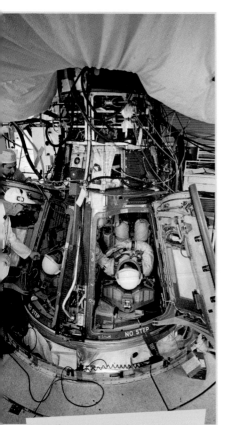

Neil Armstrong (left) and David Scott (right) get into position in Gemini 8 prior to liftoff.

LAUNCH AND CHASE

At 10:00 a.m. on March 16, 1966, NASA launched an unmanned spacecraft, the Gemini Agena Target Vehicle. One hour and 41 minutes later, Gemini 8 blasted into space carrying two astronauts. Both launches were successful, and both crafts went into orbit around Earth.

Months of planning had gone into this mission. Gemini 8 planned to chase the Agena and catch up with it. Command Pilot Neil Armstrong's job was to maneuver Gemini 8 into position to dock with the Agena. When that happened, he would attempt to dock the two vehicles. Once Gemini 8 and the Agena were linked, Dave Scott would begin his two-hour spacewalk. If all went well, Gemini 8 would release the Agena and dock a second time during the three-day mission.

First, Gemini 8 had to catch up with the Agena. Both crafts were traveling at about 18,000 miles (29,000 km) per hour. That's 10 times faster than a speeding bullet. The Agena was going slightly slower. After four orbits around Earth, Gemini 8 caught up with Agena.

Gemini 8 launched from Cape Kennedy Air Force Station, now called Cape Canaveral Air Force Station.

"WE ARE DOCKED"

Neil Armstrong corrected the path of Gemini 8 as needed. The astronauts spotted the silver rocket ahead. Radar showed that the two ships were perfectly in line. Armstrong gently approached it. "We are docked," Scott told Mission Control.

Everyone at Mission Control cheered.

Gemini 8, still docked with the Agena, moved out of communication range. Twenty-seven minutes after docking, something went wrong. The two ships, still connected, began spinning.

Agena Target Vehicle as seen from Gemini 8 before docking

While Armstrong worked to control the spin, Scott turned off various switches controlling the Agena. Nothing helped. The men suspected the Agena had caused the spin, so Scott pushed the undock button. Armstrong backed Gemini 8 away from Agena.

It didn't help. In fact, Gemini 8 started spinning even faster.

Mission Control was stunned when they heard Scott say, "We have serious problems here. We're tumbling end over end."

Armstrong added, "We're rolling up and we can't turn anything off." Gemini 8 spun faster and faster. It turned at the rate of one full revolution per second.

The spinning made Armstrong and Scott dizzy. Their vision blurred, complicating the situation, but they had only seconds to act. If the spinning continued, the astronauts would soon be unconscious and unable to fire the rockets for reentry. They would die in space.

SHUT DOWN

"All we've got left is the reentry control system," Armstrong told Mission Control.

"Press on," was the response.

Armstrong fired the 16 reentry thrusters. The spinning stopped. He steadied the spacecraft and turned off some parts of the reentry control system to save fuel. When he reactivated the maneuver thrusters, he discovered the problem. Roll thruster #8 had short-circuited and become stuck open. It had been firing continuously.

REENTRY

Firing the reentry thrusters had used up three-quarters of the fuel needed for reentry. Gemini 8 was no longer spinning, but it was now short of fuel.

Mission Control ordered an emergency landing. There would be no spacewalk and no further attempt to dock with the Agena. Gemini 8 would land three days ahead of schedule in a remote location. It wasn't ideal, but the goal was to get the astronauts home safely.

Gemini 8 was supposed to land in the Atlantic Ocean. However, the fuel shortage called for a new plan. NASA chose a secondary landing site in the Pacific Ocean about 500 miles (800 km) east of Japan. Mission Control radioed the U.S. Navy destroyer USS *Leonard Mason* to sail toward the new landing zone. Several Air Force planes raced to the area.

Gemini 8 was flying over Africa when Armstrong got the order to fire his retrorockets to initiate landing. An onboard computer guided the astronauts. Scott looked out the spacecraft window at the Himalaya Mountains. When he finally saw the blue of the ocean, he relaxed. Gemini 8 splashed down within 2 miles (3.2 km) of the revised landing spot. What was to be a three-day flight had lasted just 10 hours and 41 minutes.

RESCUE

Armstrong and Scott completed their postlanding checks as they waited for rescue. It didn't take long. Three Air Force rescuers parachuted out of an airplane and attached a flotation collar to Gemini 8. They helped Scott and Armstrong out of the spacecraft. As the group waited for the Navy ship, they bounced in the rough waves. After spinning through space, it was the ocean that gave the astronauts motion sickness.

When they finally climbed aboard the USS *Leonard Mason*, they greeted the sailors with waves and smiles. Then they headed to the sick bay to get out of their pressure suits, clean up, and get quick medical checks. They were safe and in good health.

Armstrong (right) and Scott (left) waited for the arrival of the recovery ship with the aid of U.S. Navy divers.

AGENA

Gemini 8's mission was over, but the Agena continued its orbit around Earth. Once Armstrong undocked the Gemini and Agena, Mission Control took over handling the Agena. Fifty years later, a photographer managed to capture a photo of the Agena, which was still orbiting Earth.

Despite the problems with the mission, Gemini 8 proved that two vehicles could meet, dock in space, and undock successfully. Neil Armstrong regained control of his spacecraft during the emergency, proving his ability as a pilot. Thanks to NASA's careful arrangement for a Pacific Ocean landing, the astronauts came back safely. In his book about the Gemini program, Gus Grissom wrote, "This was as close as United States astronauts came to a catastrophic situation during the whole of the Gemini program."

THE RESULTS

NASA experts investigated, but they never found a reason why roll thruster #8 became stuck open. However, they did make important changes to future Gemini crafts to avoid similar problems. For example, they added a master switch that allowed astronauts to turn off pieces of equipment one at a time to determine what part of the system wasn't working correctly.

Gemini 8 clearly proved Neil Armstrong's ability as a space pilot. His quick thinking and calm manner saved the day. The flight highlighted the many dangers of space flight. As Grissom wrote, "Gemini 8 reminded the public, briefly, that spaceflight was not yet as simple as a ride on a trolley car."

Astronauts Neil Armstrong and Buzz Aldrin placed a U.S. flag on the moon.

DID YOU KNOW?

Neil Armstrong served as a Navy pilot from 1949 to 1952 and became an astronaut in 1962. Gemini 8 was his first spaceflight. Later, he assumed command of Apollo 11, the first manned mission to the moon. On July 20, 1969, he became the first human to step onto the moon's surface.

STRANDED!
A STORY OF APOLLO

In 1969 NASA workers dropped an oxygen tank they had removed from Apollo 10 for maintenance. It dropped from a height of just 2 inches (5 centimeters). The tank was inspected, and when no damage was found, it was reused in Apollo 13. A year later, that dropped tank led to a disaster that captured the attention of millions of TV viewers who waited breathlessly to see if the men of Apollo 13 would survive.

Commander Jim Lovell and his crew of Fred Haise and Jack Swigert were headed for the moon when they blasted off on April 11, 1970. They had spent years preparing for a moon landing, but Apollo 13 never made it that far.

OFF TO A GOOD START

The first two days of the mission were among the smoothest of the Apollo program. At 46 hours and 43 minutes Mission Control told the crew, "The spacecraft is in real good shape as far as we are concerned. We're bored to tears down here."

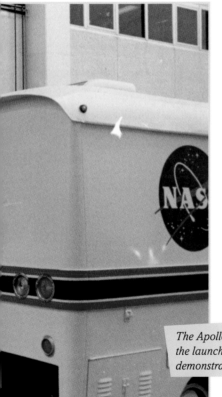

The crew relaxed. They completed a TV broadcast designed to show viewers on Earth how they lived and worked in the weightlessness of space. Jim Lovell ended the show saying, "This is the crew of Apollo 13 wishing everybody there a nice evening. . . . Good night." The astronauts expected a nice evening too, but it wasn't to be.

The Apollo 13 crew headed to the launch site for a countdown demonstration test.

THE EXPLOSION

Nine minutes after the TV broadcast, Mission Control noticed a low-pressure warning signal on one of the ship's hydrogen tanks. That sometimes happened when the tanks needed to be stirred. The procedure, called a cryo stir, stopped the super-cold gases from dividing into layers. Ground controllers notified the crew that it was time to perform the stir.

Jack Swigert flipped the switch to begin the cryo stir.

Seconds later the spacecraft shuddered. Alarms went off, the oxygen pressure fell, and the power went out.

Swigert called Mission Control. "Houston, we've had a problem here."

"This is Houston. Say again, please."

A minute later Lovell looked out the window. "We are venting something out into the—into space. It's a gas of some sort."

As soon as he saw that leak, Lovell knew that the mission to the moon was over. He later wrote, "The knot tightened in my stomach, and all regrets about not landing on the moon vanished. Now it was strictly a case of survival."

What Lovell had seen was oxygen leaking out of tank #1. He didn't realize what it was at the time, nor did he know that neither oxygen tank in the service module was functional. Tank #2 had exploded and then sucked the oxygen out of tank #1.

POWER PROBLEMS

Lovell checked the gauges again. They indicated that the oxygen tanks were empty, and the spacecraft was losing power. There was a backup oxygen supply on board, but the explosion had also knocked out two of the three fuel cells. The fuel cells provided the electricity to power the ship. They also combined hydrogen and oxygen to produce water. The spacecraft's systems required water to keep them cool, and the crew used it for drinking, washing, and preparing food.

Mission Control suggested turning off one valve and then another. They powered down the fuel cells and then shut them down. But nothing seemed to stop the leak or increase the pressure. It was clear to Mission Control that Apollo 13 had suffered serious damage. Without power or water, the spacecraft was in trouble.

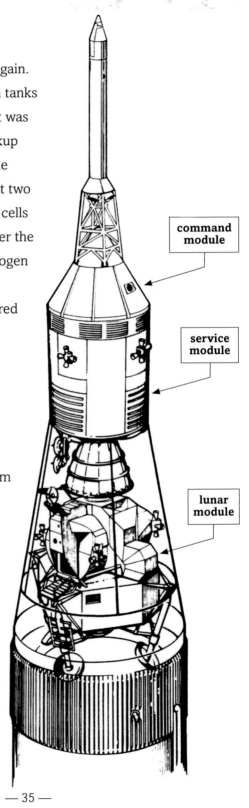

command module

service module

lunar module

Apollo 13 spacecraft in its launch configuration

THE LIFEBOAT

Mission Control told the crew, "We are starting to think about the LM [lunar module] lifeboat."

"That's what we have been thinking about too," Swigert said, speaking for the crew.

The LM still had power and oxygen. It had water too—at least enough to last for a short time. Lovell and Haise made their way to the LM. Swigert stayed in the command module for a few minutes to finish some chores. The command module had only 15 minutes of power left.

The Apollo 13 team at Mission Control works on a device for the crew to copy in the spacecraft to solve the oxygen problem.

The LM was built for two men, not three. Once Swigert arrived, the space was crowded. The LM had a 45-hour supply of oxygen, power, and water. But it would take at least twice that, nearly four days, to bring the astronauts home.

SCRAMBLING

NASA scientists and engineers made rapid-fire decisions about how to get the astronauts home. Thousands of people with technical skills worked on the problems in places as far apart as Florida, Massachusetts, Wisconsin, and California. They calculated the amount of power the spacecraft needed and where to get that power. They wrote new procedures, tested them, and then passed them along to the Apollo 13 crew. The crew members reduced power needs as much as possible. They had to save power for reentry to get home.

The ship continued to travel toward the moon, which was about 20 hours distant. They were 200,000 miles (320,000 km) from home.

SHIVERING, TIRED, AND THIRSTY

In the LM, the astronauts cut power as much as possible. Only the life-support system stayed on. They had enough oxygen, but water was the big problem. The astronauts allotted 6 ounces (177 milliliters) per person each day. That's one-fifth of the average water intake. They supplemented the water with fruit juices. Even so, they became dehydrated.

The astronauts ate hot dogs and other wetpack foods when they ate at all. Much of the food on board had to be mixed with hot water, which they couldn't spare. But they were too tired to eat much anyway. Jim Lovell lost 14 pounds (6.4 kg) on the mission. The three-member crew lost a total of 31.5 pounds (14 kg), 50 percent more than any other Apollo crew.

Living for four days in the tiny LM proved challenging. As Lovell wrote, "The trip was marked by discomfort beyond the lack of food and water. Sleep was almost impossible because of the cold. When we turned off the electrical systems, we lost our source of heat. . . . We were as cold as frogs in a frozen pool, especially Jack Swigert, who got his feet wet and didn't have lunar overshoes. It wasn't simply that the temperature dropped to 38°F (3.3°C): the sight of perspiring walls and wet windows made it seem even colder. We considered putting on our spacesuits, but they would have been bulky and too sweaty. Our Teflon-coated inflight coveralls were cold to the touch, and how we longed for some good old thermal underwear."

After the astronauts had spent a day and a half in the LM, a warning light showed that the carbon dioxide level was climbing. Breathing too much carbon dioxide is deadly. The command module had carbon dioxide filters, but the filters didn't work in the lunar module. Experts at Mission Control came up with a solution using plastic bags, cardboard, and tape from the spacecraft. The crew followed Mission Control's instructions to put it together. It worked!

AROUND THE MOON

Turning the ship around for a quick return to Earth was too risky. After all, the engine might have been damaged in the explosion. It was safer to continue on its path to the moon and then circle it. After that, Apollo 13 would head home.

Firing the LM's descent engine for a 35-second burst put Apollo 13 back on its planned course around the moon. The descent engine was designed to carry Lovell and Haise to the moon, but that wasn't going to happen.

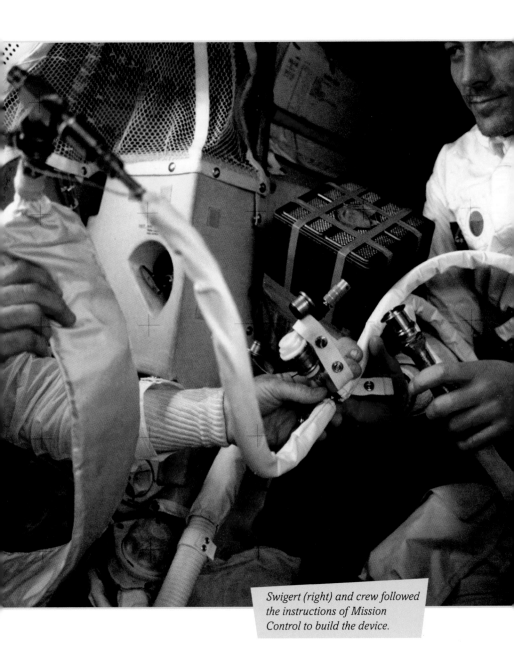

Swigert (right) and crew followed the instructions of Mission Control to build the device.

On the night of April 14, Apollo 13 reached the dark side of the moon. The crew was a record distance away and out of radio contact—249,205 miles (401,057 km) from Earth. At one point, they were only 164 miles (264 km) from the moon's surface. Haise and Swigert took photos. They didn't know that billions of people were following their flight on radio, TV, and in newspapers.

NASA announced that if everything worked as planned, Apollo 13 would splash down in the Pacific Ocean, north of New Zealand. World leaders offered help. The Soviet Union, France, and Britain sent ships to the proposed recovery area in case they could be of help. The world watched and waited, praying that the astronauts would return safely.

Apollo 13 took pictures of the far side of the moon, capturing an image of Tsiolovsky crater.

NAVIGATING

Mission Control told Lovell he would have to fire the engines again after the spacecraft rounded the moon. Apollo 13 didn't drive itself. Lovell, as pilot, had to determine the exact right course.

Normally, he would have used the stars the way sailors used to do at sea. A computer would then help him line up the course. But he couldn't find a real star to use. Debris from the explosion glinted in the sun like stars. Lovell called them "false stars." Finally, Dorothy Johnson, an expert at Mission Control, suggested using the sun as a guide. It worked. Lovell set his course relying on the sun.

Two hours after rounding the moon, NASA asked Lovell to fire the engines again. This burn lasted five minutes and reduced the time needed to get home.

HEADING HOME

Apollo 13 was now headed in the right direction, but unfortunately, the problems weren't over. The astronauts were still in the lunar module, but they couldn't use it for the landing because it had no heat shield. Without a heat shield, it would burn up when it reentered Earth's atmosphere. The astronauts wouldn't survive. They had to get back into the command module.

As Apollo 13 approached Earth, Mission Control sent more instructions. The crew released the service module into space. It floated away, and the crew looked out the window and saw the damage for the first time. One entire panel had blown away. No wonder the ship shuddered when the oxygen tank exploded.

Powering up the CM (command module) usually took days, not hours. Mission Control devised a new plan to power up the CM quickly. With the power back on, the crew moved out of the LM and into the CM. It was cold, dark, and wet. Everything was covered with droplets of water that kept dripping as if it were raining inside.

Finally, the astronauts released the lunar module. They sent their "lifeboat" into space and prepared for splashdown.

Apollo 13 landed in the Pacific Ocean, only a few miles from the predicted landing spot. The crew was thrilled to be home. And they were surprised to find that so many people had been following their journey and praying for their safe return. People around the world cheered and cried in relief.

The *Iwo Jima*, a Navy aircraft carrier, picked them up. The crew then traveled to Hawaii, where their wives and families were waiting. So was President Richard Nixon.

CHANGES

Lovell later wrote, ". . . without the splendid people in Mission Control, and their backups, we'd still be up there. However, I would be remiss not to state that it really was the teamwork between the ground and flight crew that resulted in a successful return. I was blessed with two shipmates who were very knowledgeable about their spacecraft systems."

Lovell called the mission "a successful failure." Not only did the men return safely, but NASA also made many changes that helped future missions. What had earlier been considered a slight mishap—the dropping of

the oxygen tank before the mission—caused the slight damage that led to the explosion. After Apollo 13, improvements were made in the way oxygen tanks were handled, stored, and stirred. NASA also added extra batteries and water storage bags for the crew to use in emergency situations.

The Apollo 13 accident became the basis for a movie of the same name in 1995. While the movie isn't 100 percent accurate, it shows the courage and clear thinking of the astronauts and their helpers on the ground.

Swigert was lifted from the command module by helicopter while Lovell and a U.S. Navy diver waited below.

COLLISION!
A STORY OF MIR

The Soviet Union launched the Mir space station in February 1986. Mir was designed as a place for astronauts to live in space while conducting experiments and research. In 1992 the United States joined the project. Mir hosted astronauts from both countries. At first, Mir consisted of primary living and working areas. These contained life-support and power systems, as well as the main computer, communications, and control equipment. Over time, other modules were added. In May 1995 a U.S. module called Spektr joined Mir. It contained living quarters for U.S. astronauts and two pairs of solar arrays to boost Mir's power systems.

NASA astronaut Jerry Linenger compared Mir to "six school buses all hooked together. It was as if four of the buses were driven into a four-way intersection at the same time. They collided and became attached. All at right angles to each other, these four buses made up the four Mir science modules."

American astronauts traveled to the Mir on the space shuttle Soyuz. Progress supply vessels, which were unmanned, carried supplies to Mir about three times a year. They docked with Mir to allow astronauts and supplies to transfer to the space station.

A TEST

Mir was built to last for five years. By 1997 it had been in use for 11 years. During that time the former Soviet Union had broken up. Russia, formerly part of the Soviet Union, continued the space program. When Mir's docking system developed problems, the Russian Space Agency decided to test a backup system. That decision nearly cost the lives of the three astronauts on board.

The plan seemed simple enough. Mir's crew would fill the Progress vessel with garbage so that it weighed as much as a supply ship. Then they would send it into space, turn it around, and dock it again with Mir. The mission wasn't about garbage. It was about testing the backup docking system.

Completed in 1986, Russian space station Mir had a greater mass than any previous spacecraft.

DID YOU KNOW?

In the Russian language, *mir* means "world," "peace," and "village." No one word in English quite matches the meaning.

WHERE'S PROGRESS?

On June 25, 1997, Vasily Tsibliyev, Mir's Russian commander, performed the test. He sent Progress into space, turned it around, and prepared for docking. A remote camera filmed Progress as it approached Mir. From the space station, Tsibliyev watched on a small TV screen as Progress approached and used two joysticks to control the vessel. On a previous attempt, the monitor hadn't worked correctly. Tsibliyev doubted it would ever work, but he followed orders and tried again.

Russian Ground Control turned off the radar because the ground control workers thought it might have caused the earlier problems. Tsibliyev would have to depend on the picture he saw on the TV monitor. But when he looked at the screen, all he saw was static. Where was the Progress? How fast it was going?

The other astronauts on board, American Michael Foale and Russian Aleksander Lazutkin, peered out the window looking for Progress. Clouds and the solar panels on Mir blocked their view. Foale was at work in Spektr at the time. By the time he spotted Progress, it was headed directly for Mir, and it was going too fast.

CRASH!

Tsibliyev fired the braking-rocket. Progress didn't slow down.

Lazutkin later said that Progress looked "full of menace, like a shark. I watched this black body covered in spots sliding past below me. I looked closer, and at that point there was a great thump and the whole station shook."

Foale said, "I felt through my fingers a shudder, a thump on the station, and I heard what seemed to be far off, like a thump. At that point, I knew we had been hit by the Progress."

Progress slammed into Spektr. It tore a hole in one of the solar panels, crumpled a radiator, and damaged the hull. The air pressure inside Mir began to fall, and the station began spinning. Both were serious problems.

DAMAGE CONTROL

The hole in Spektr's hull meant a loss of air, and if enough air were lost, the crew wouldn't survive. The radiator dumped heat from Mir's electrical system into space to keep the station from overheating. The situation was critical, a battle of life or death. The crew members had to calculate how much time they had left. If they didn't solve the problems within 30 minutes, they would have to abandon Mir and escape in the Soyuz, still docked at Mir.

Michael Foale was working in the mid-deck of the station before the collision.

However, they had no intention of leaving without trying to fix Mir. They cut various power cables, which allowed them to close the hatch and seal off Spektr. They were no longer losing air, but they were still spinning. It wasn't an end-over-end spin like Gemini 8, but it meant that Mir's solar panels no longer faced the sun. Without sun, there was no power.

Tsibliyev (left) and his crew headed to the Soyuz launch that took them to Mir in January 1997.

POWER FAILURE

The main computer shut down. The lights switched off. Mir lost radio contact with Earth. The only sound was that of the astronauts' breathing.

The crew worked in darkness to assess the damage. They mopped up the condensation dripping down the walls while Mir continued to spin. They could communicate with Earth only briefly when the solar panels faced the sun during their spin.

To determine a course of action to stop the spin, Mission Control needed to know how fast Mir was spinning. Without computers available, Foale had to use his knowledge of the stars to estimate the speed of the spin. He went to the window and held his thumb up against the field of stars to make a rough calculation. Mir was spinning at about one degree per second. Using Foale's estimate, Mission Control instructed the crew on how to fire Mir's engine to counteract the spin. It didn't stop the spin completely, but it was just enough to regain their power. Over the next several weeks, the astronauts regained 70 percent power.

Spektr was never repaired, and its many experiments were abandoned. The Progress was sent back into space, where it and its load of garbage burned up.

Mir lasted until 2001, when it was disposed of in the Pacific Ocean to avoid creating more space junk. The International Space Station (ISS) replaced Mir. ISS uses a more advanced docking program to prevent similar incidents. Despite the more than 8,000 man-made objects currently in Earth's orbit—and hundreds of thousands more space junk pieces—there has never been another life-threatening collision.

The solar panels on the Spektr module showed damage after the docking collision.

DROWNING IN SPACE?
A STORY OF THE INTERNATIONAL SPACE STATION

The International Space Station (ISS) is a joint venture of the United States, Russia, Canada, Japan, Brazil, and the European Space Agency, which includes 11 European countries. The Space Station was built in low Earth orbit beginning in 1998. It became operational in 2000 and continues to host astronauts from around the world.

Italian Luca Parmitano joined the European Space Agency in 2009. On May 28, 2013, he made the six-hour flight to the station on Russia's Soyuz spacecraft. He joined five other astronauts on the ISS, who were grouped into teams called expeditions. Parmitano's team was Expedition 36. Other members of Expedition 36 and 37 were Commander Pavel Vinogradov, Fyodor Yurchikhin, and Alexander Misurkin of Russia, and Chris Cassidy and Karen Nyberg of the United States.

At 7:57 a.m. on July 16, 2013, Cassidy and Parmitano prepared to work outside the station. This was their second spacewalk in eight days. During the earlier spacewalk, Parmitano became the first Italian to walk in space. During the second, he nearly died.

SPACEWALKING

In the 1990s, when NASA was planning the space station, experts worried about the dangers posed by EVAs (Extravehicular Activity) or spacewalks. Any time astronauts stepped outside the protective environment of the space station, they faced dangers. But over time, EVAs became less worrisome. In fact, there had been 170 previous spacewalks to build and repair the space station without a single serious accident. Spacewalking seemed almost routine and safe.

Astronauts say spacewalking is an unforgettable experience. NASA astronaut Mike Foreman described it in a 2015 interview. "When you put on that spacesuit and go outside, you're weightless. You have beautiful views of the Earth, of the stars, of the outside of the space station; it's just an amazing feeling."

A week earlier Parmitano hadn't been sure how he'd react during his first spacewalk as he dangled 250 miles (400 km) above Earth. It turned out that he loved it.

The International Space Station orbits Earth about every 90 minutes.

WORKING WITH CASSIDY

Parmitano and Cassidy worked outside the shuttle for six hours. They moved some equipment, checked experiments, and prepared power and data cables for a new Russian module scheduled to arrive soon. They planned to continue that work on their second spacewalk. Parmitano said later, "If you watch him [Cassidy], you think, *This is easy, I can do that.* Well, let me tell you, the environment we work in is incredibly harsh. It will kill you if you make mistakes."

Parmitano's first spacewalk had one small problem. At least, it seemed small at the time. Some water leaked into Parmitano's helmet. Space station officials and the astronauts decided a leaky drink bag attached to the front of the spacesuit was the likely cause. If astronauts get thirsty, they open a valve and suck on the tube to get water. Parmitano replaced the drink bag.

THE SECOND SPACEWALK

On July 16 Parmitano and Cassidy squeezed into their Extravehicular Mobility Units (EMUs) for a second spacewalk. Parmitano left the airlock first. He was excited. Parmitano wrote about the experience when he returned to Earth. Before the walk, he felt "fully charged, as if electricity and not blood were running through my veins."

He attached two 85-foot (26-m) safety tethers to the space station, one for Cassidy and one for himself. Cassidy followed, and the two men checked each other before starting work on their assigned projects. The work was going well. In fact, Parmitano and Cassidy were ahead of schedule when Parmitano felt that something was wrong.

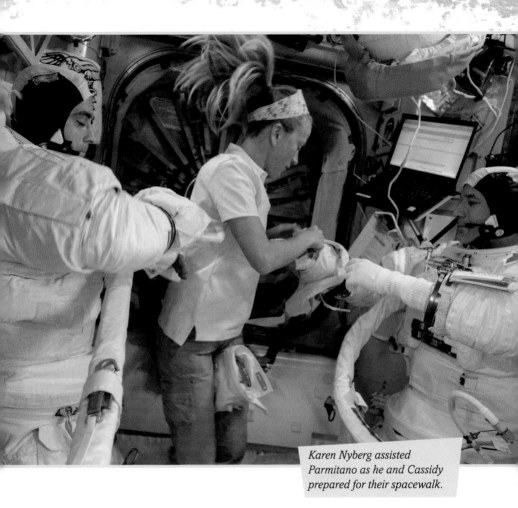

Karen Nyberg assisted Parmitano as he and Cassidy prepared for their spacewalk.

DID YOU KNOW?

The spacesuits used by shuttle astronauts, called EMUs (Extravehicular Mobility Units), have two oxygen tanks to allow for a six- to eight-and-a-half-hour spacewalk. EMUs protect astronauts from the zero pressure and extreme temperatures of space, which can range from −250° to 250°F (−157° to 121°C).

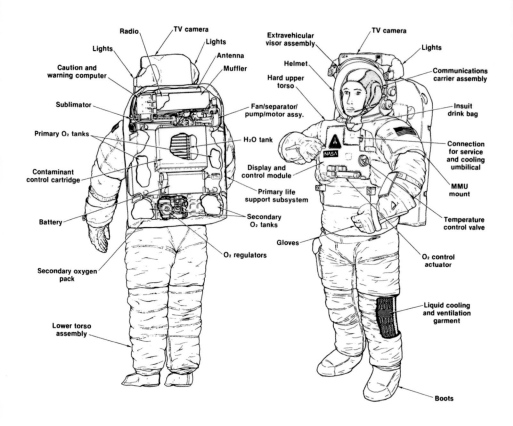

Radio · TV camera · Lights · Extravehicular visor assembly · TV camera
Lights · Antenna · Helmet · Lights
Caution and warning computer · Muffler · Communications carrier assembly
Hard upper torso
Sublimator · Fan/separator/pump/motor assy. · Insuit drink bag
Primary O₂ tanks · H₂O tank · Connection for service and cooling umbilical
Display and control module
Contaminant control cartridge · MMU mount
Primary life support subsystem
Battery · Secondary O₂ tanks · Temperature control valve
Gloves
O₂ regulators · O₂ control actuator
Secondary oxygen pack · Liquid cooling and ventilation garment
Lower torso assembly
Boots

Extravehicular Mobility Unit (EMU)

WATER AGAIN?

Parmitano later wrote in his journal, "The unexpected sensation of water at the back of my neck surprises me—and I'm in a place where I'd rather not be surprised. I move my head from side to side, confirming my first impression, and with superhuman effort I force myself to inform Houston of what I can feel, knowing that it could signal the end of this EVA."

Cassidy moved to where Parmitano was working to see if he could find the source of the leak. Could it be the drink bag again? Maybe it was sweat. EVAs require lots of effort, and it's not unusual for astronauts to work up a sweat. But Parmitano's drink bag wasn't leaking, and the water was cold, not warm like sweat would be. Parmitano was alarmed because the water inside his helmet was increasing.

TERMINATE!

Mission Control decided to end the spacewalk. They sent word to Parmitano and Cassidy. They told Cassidy to secure the equipment outside the station and then make his way back to the airlock. They told Parmitano to go back immediately. Cassidy hated to leave Parmitano, but he had work to do. The men separated, and Parmitano was on his own.

As Parmitano made his way to the airlock, he felt the water increasing. It covered the sponges on his earphones. Without the earphones, he feared losing contact with Cassidy, the ISS astronauts, and Mission Control.

Water kept flowing into Parmitano's helmet. In space, without gravity, the water congealed into a spherical shape or blob. It hovered at the front of the helmet's visor and blurred his vision. The sun was setting. Darkness, combined with the water covering his eyes, would soon make it impossible to see. Parmitano tried to remain calm, but he was out in space, losing the use of his ears and his eyes. Could it get worse?

UPSIDE DOWN

As he worked his way toward the airlock, Parmitano realized that he would have to flip upside down to allow his safety cable to unwind. The blob of water had grown larger and covered his nose, threatening his airway. Parmitano shook his head, but that only made things worse. He later wrote, "By now, the upper part of the helmet is full of water and I can't even be sure that the next time I breathe I will fill my lungs with air and not liquid. To make matters worse, I realize that I can't even understand which direction I should head in to get back to the airlock. I can't see more than a few centimeters in front of me, not even enough to make out the handles we use to move around the station."

THE DECISION

The water made it impossible for Parmitano to hear Cassidy, and he suspected that no one could hear him either. He couldn't hear, couldn't see, and soon he wouldn't be able to breathe. He felt utterly alone. If he waited where he was, he knew Cassidy would come to get him. But would he still be alive by then?

Parmitano forced himself to remain calm. He began working out a plan. First he had to reach the airlock. Then if the water blob continued to grow and covered his mouth, he would open a valve on the helmet to let some of the water out. Otherwise, if the water blob reached his mouth, he would drown when he tried to breathe. Opening the valve on the helmet might cause him to pass out because of the loss of pressure, but at least he wouldn't drown.

Parmitano's plan would only work if he was already inside the airlock and the airlock was closed. He remembered his safety cable. He used it to pull himself to the airlock. He peered through the water in his helmet and was relieved to see the airlock. He managed to get back inside and wait there for Cassidy, who arrived soon after and closed the hatch.

Parmitano works on a computer in the Destiny laboratory of the ISS.

INSIDE HELP

American astronaut Karen Nyberg listened to the conversation between Mission Control and the astronauts. As soon as Parmitano and Cassidy were safely inside, she began repressurizing the airlock. Parmitano and Cassidy couldn't enter the station until the pressure was equalized, which took several minutes.

Parmitano wrote later, "I try to move as little as possible to avoid moving the water inside my helmet. . . . Now that we are repressurizing, I know that if the water does overwhelm me I can always open the helmet. I'll probably lose consciousness, but in any case that would be better than drowning inside the helmet. At one point, Chris squeezes my glove with his and I give him the universal 'ok' sign with mine."

When the airlock opened, Nyberg removed Parmitano's helmet. Up to a liter of water gushed out.

CLOSE CALL

NASA investigated. In their report they wrote, "EV2's [Parmitano's] calm demeanor in the face of his helmet filling with water possibly saved his life." The team's chairman added, "I would say of all the EVA issues we've encountered to date, this is probably the most serious." NASA concluded that "a water separation pump—part of the suit's cooling system—became clogged, causing water to back up and flow into the suit's air vents."

Parmitano hasn't let his close call discourage him from additional spaceflight. A month after the incident, he wrote, "Space is a harsh, inhospitable frontier and we are explorers, not colonizers. The skills of our engineers and the technology surrounding us make things appear simple when they are not, and perhaps we forget this sometimes."

He adds that it's "better not to forget."

Cassidy (left) and Parmitano (right) in a new module a month after Parmitano's spacewalk incident

DID YOU KNOW?

Teams of astronauts continue to live and work on the ISS for various periods of time. They manage about 100 experiments in multiple laboratories on the space station. Many of the experiments investigate the effect of weightlessness on human beings and other living things.

GLOSSARY

atmosphere—the layer of gases that surrounds Earth and some other planets and moons

atmospheric pressure—the pressure caused by the weight of the atmosphere, which allows people to breathe and regulates gases within the body

cosmonaut—an astronaut of the Russian or Soviet space program

decompression sickness—an illness brought on by a rapid decrease of pressure that causes muscle and joint pain, nausea, numbness, and paralysis

dock—to link up or connect

drogue chute—a parachute designed to slow a rapidly moving object, provide stability, or deploy a larger parachute

filter—a device that cleans liquids or gases that pass through it

fuel cell—a device that produces electrical power on a spacecraft

low Earth orbit—an orbit around Earth with an altitude of 1,200 miles (2,000 km) or less

module—a separate component or part of a larger system

NASA—National Aeronautics and Space Administration, the agency that runs the U.S. space program

orbit—the curved path around a planet, star, or moon

repressurize—to increase the pressure in an enclosed space, such as an airlock, to match atmospheric pressure

solar array—a large-scale electrical device made by combining several solar panels

Soviet Union—a former federation (1922–1991) of 15 republics that included Russia, Ukraine, and other nations of eastern Europe and northern Asia; also called the Union of Soviet Socialist Republics (USSR)

suborbital—not in orbit

tether—a rope or cable used to limit the range of motion

thruster—a small rocket attached to a spacecraft used to control its motion or direction; different kinds of thrusters serve different purposes, such as the ones saved for reentry

wetpack foods—packaged food that requires no water to be added before eating

READ MORE

Krumm, Brian. *Shuttle in the Sky: The Columbia Disaster*. North Mankato, MN: Capstone Press, 2016.

Rissman, Rebecca. *Houston, We've Had a Problem: The Story of the Apollo 13 Disaster*. North Mankato, MN: Capstone Press, 2018.

Zoehfeld, Kathleen Weidner. *Apollo 13: How Three Brave Astronauts Survived a Space Disaster*. New York: Random House, 2015.

INTERNET SITES

Gemini 8: NASA's First Docking in Pictures
https://www.space.com/39765-gemini-8-mission-first-space-docking-photos.html

Italian Astronaut Recounts Near-Drowning in Spacesuit
https://www.space.com/22485-italian-astronaut-spacesuit-leak-video.html

NASA for Students, Grades 5–8
https://www.nasa.gov/audience/forstudents/index.html

Smithsonian National Air and Space Museum:
The Apollo Program
https://airandspace.si.edu/explore-and-learn/topics/apollo/apollo-program/

SOURCE NOTES

p. 7,"Liftoff was very smooth..." Virgil "Gus" Grissom. *Gemini: A Personal Account of Man's Venture into Space*. New York: The Macmillan Company, 1968, p. 288-2899.

p. 7, "seemed jet black" Ibid., p. 290.

p. 9, "All I could see was blue sky..." Ibid., p. 295.

p. 10, "This was the best thing..." Ibid., p. 294.

p. 12, "I wasn't scared now..." Ibid., p. 296-297.

p. 12, "I had to swim hard..." Ibid., p. 297.

p. 13, "The conquest of space..." Mary White, "Detailed Biographies of Apollo I Crew - Gus Grissom," NASA, August 4, 2006, history.nasa.gov/Apollo204/zorn/grissom.htm Accessed on March 19, 2019.

p. 15, "like a seagull..." Alexei Leonov, "The Nightmare of Voshkod2," *Air and Space*, January 2005, https://www. mag.com/space/the-nightmare-of-voskhod-2-8655378/ Accessed on March 19, 2019.

p. 16, "My feet had pulled away..." Ibid.

p. 16, "It was taking far longer..." Mike McKinnon, "50 Years Ago, the First Spacewalk Nearly Ended in Tragedy," *Gizmodo*, March 18, 2015, gizmodo.com/50-years-ago-the-first-spacewalk-nearly-ended-in-trage-1692303108 Accessed on March 19, 2019.

p. 19, "We can make only one..." "The Nightmare of Voshkod2."

p. 20, "We heard them roar..." Ibid.

p. 26, "We are docked" Bob Granath, "Gemini's First Docking Turns to Wild Ride in Orbit," NASA, March 3, 2016, www.nasa.gov/feature/geminis-first-docking-turns-to-wild-ride-in-orbit Accessed on March 19, 2019.

p. 27, "We have serious problems..." Ibid.

p. 27, "We're rolling up..." Ibid.

p. 27, "All we've got left..." Larry Merritt, "The Abbreviated Flight of Gemini 8," *Boeing Frontiers Online*, March 2006, www.boeing.com/news/frontiers/archive/2006/march/i_history.html Accessed on March 19, 2019.

p. 27, "Press on" Ibid.

p. 30, "This was as close as United States..." *Gemini: A Personal Account*, p. 155.

p. 30, "Gemini 8 reminded..." Ibid., p. 158.

p. 33, "The spacecraft is in real good shape..." "Apollo 13," NASA, July 8, 2009, www.nasa.gov/mission_pages/apollo/missions/apollo13.html Accessed on March 19, 2019.

p. 33, "This is the crew of Apollo 13..." Ibid.

p. 34, "Houston, we've had a problem..." Ibid.

p. 34, "This is Houston..." W D. Woods et al., "Apollo 13: Day 3, Houston We've Had a Problem," *Apollo Flight Journal*, NASA, 2015, https://history.nasa.gov/afj/ap13fj/08day3-problem.html Accessed on March 19, 2019.

p. 34, "The knot tightened..." James Lovell, "Apollo Expeditions to the Moon: Houston We've Had a Problem," NASA, history.nasa.gov/SP-350/ch-13-2.html Accessed on March 19, 2019.

p. 36, "We're starting to think..." "Apollo 13: Day 3."

p. 36, "That's what we have been..." Ibid.

p. 38, "The trip was marked..." "Apollo Expeditions to the Moon."

p. 42, "a successful failure..." Ibid.

p. 44, "six school buses..." "MIR Space Station," NASA, history.nasa.gov/SP-4225/mir/mir.htm Accessed on March 19, 2019.

p. 46, "full of menace..." "Progress Collision with MIR Animation," NASA, history.nasa.gov/SP-4225/multimedia/progress-collision.htm Accessed on March 19, 2019.

p. 46, "I felt through my fingers..." "MIR Space Station Collision," YouTube, September 3, 2007, www.youtube.com/watch?time_continue=515&v=tM7fTLLmgbk Accessed on March 19, 2019.

p. 51, "When you put on that spacesuit..." Olivia Rudgard, "Spacewalking: What's It Like to Float 250 Miles above Earth?" *The Telegraph*, June 3, 2015, www.telegraph.co.uk/news/science/space/11647899/Spacewalking-Whats-it-like-to-float-250-miles-above-earth.html Accessed on March 19, 2019.

p. 52, "If you watch him..." Tony Reichhardt, "The Spacewalk that Almost Killed Him," *Air and Space*, May 2014, www.airspacemag.com/space/spacewalk-almost-killed-him-180950135/?all Accessed on March 19, 2019.

p. 52, "fully charged..." Luca Parmitano, "EVA 23: Exploring the Frontier," ESA (European Space Agency), August 20, 2013, http://blogs.esa.int/luca-parmitano/2013/08/20/eva-23-exploring-the-frontier/ Accessed on March 19, 2019.

p. 54, "The unexpected sensation of water..." Ibid.

p. 56, "By now, the upper part..." Ibid.

p. 58, "I try to move as little as possible..." Ibid.

p. 58, "EV2's [Parmitano's] calm demeanor..." *New Scientist*, March 8, 2014, p. 6.

p. 58 Space is a harsh..." "EVA 23: Exploring the Frontier."

SELECT BIBLIOGRAPHY

Books

Grissom, Virgil "Gus." *Gemini: A Personal Account of Man's Venture into Space.* New York: The Macmillan Company, 1968.

Grissom, Virgil I. *We Seven: By the Astronauts Themselves.* New York: Simon & Schuster, 1962.

Websites and Articles

"Apollo 13," NASA, July 8, 2009, www.nasa.gov/mission_pages/apollo/missions/apollo13.html Accessed on March 19, 2019.

Berger, Eric,"Gus Grissom taught NASA a hard lesson: 'You can hurt yourself in the ocean,'" *ars technica*, October 8, 2016, https://arstechnica.com/science/2016/11/with-every-splashdown-nasa-embraces-the-legacy-of-gus-grissom/ Accessed on March 19, 2019.

Dunn, Marcia, "Liberty Bell 7 Yields Clues to Its Sinking," *Los Angeles Times*, December 12, 1999, articles.latimes.com/1999/dec/12/news/mn-43115 Accessed on March 19, 2019.

Gelernter, Josh, "Neil Armstrong's Forgotten First Space Flight," *National Review*, March 5, 2016, www.nationalreview.com/2016/04/gemini-8-forgotten-mission-almost-ended-space-program/ Accessed on March 19, 2019.

"Gemini VIII," edited by Mark Wade, www.astronautix.com/g/gemini8.html Accessed on March 19, 2019.

Gini, Andrea, "Lessons Learned: MIR Collision," *Space Safety Magazine*, September 16, 2011, www.spacesafetymagazine.com/space-disasters/close-calls/lessons-learned-mir-collision/ Accessed on March 19, 2019.

Gordon, Michael R., "Russian Space Station Damaged in Collision with a Cargo Vessel," *New York Times*, June 26, 1997, www.nytimes.com/1997/06/26/world/russian-space-station-damaged-in-collision-with-a-cargo-vessel.html Accessed on March 19, 2019.

Granath, Bob, "Gemini's First Docking Turns to Wild Ride in Orbit," NASA, March 3, 2016, www.nasa.gov/feature/geminis-first-docking-turns-to-wild-ride-in-orbit Accessed on March 19, 2019.

Howell, Elizabeth, "Apollo 13: Facts About NASA's Near-Disaster," Space.com, October 9, 2017, www.space.com/17250-apollo-13-facts.html Accessed on March 19, 2019.

Hutchinson, Lee, "45 years after Apollo 13: Ars Look at What Went Wrong and Why," *ars technica*, April 16, 2015, https://arstechnica.com/science/2015/04/apollo-13-the-mistakes-the-explosion-and-six-hours-of-live-saving-decisions/2/ Accessed on March 19, 2019.

Kramer, Miriam, "Italian Astronaut Recounts Near-Drowning in Spacesuit (Video)," Space.com, August 27, 2018, www.space.com/22485-italian-astronaut-spacesuit-leak-video.html Accessed on March 19, 2019.

Leonov, Alexei, "The Nightmare of Voskhod2," *Air and Space*, January 2005, https://www.airspacemag.com/space/the-nightmare-of-voskhod-2-8655378/ Accessed on March 19, 2019.

Lovell, James A., "Houston, We've Had a Problem," Apollo Expeditions to the Moon, NASA, June 28, 1975, https://history.nasa.gov/SP-350/ch-13-1.html Accessed on March 19, 2019.

McKinnon, Mike, "50 Years Ago, the First Spacewalk Nearly Ended in Tragedy," *Gizmodo*, https://gizmodo.com/50-years-ago-the-first-spacewalk-nearly-ended-in-trage-1692303108 Accessed on March 19, 2019.

Merritt, Larry, "The Abbreviated Flight of Gemini 8," *Boeing Frontiers Online*, March 2006, www.boeing.com/news/frontiers/archive/2006/march/i_history.html Accessed on March 19, 2019.

"Mir Space Station," NASA, https://history.nasa.gov/SP-4225/mir/mir.htm#core Accessed on March 19, 2019.

"NASA - Mercury-Redstone 4," MERCURY: America's First Astronauts, NASA, www.nasa.gov/mission_pages/mercury/missions/libertybell7.html Accessed on March 19, 2019.

"Parmitano Goes Beyond," European Space Agency, September 27, 2018, www.esa.int/Our_Activities/Human_Spaceflight/Astronauts/Luca_Parmitano_goes_Beyond Accessed on March 19, 2019.

Paul, Rincon, "The First Spacewalk: How the First Human to Take Steps in Outer Space Nearly Didn't Return to Earth," BBC, October 13, 2014, www.bbc.co.uk/news/special/2014/newsspec_9035/index.html Accessed on March 19, 2019.

"Progress Collision with MIR Animation," NASA, https://history.nasa.gov/SP-4225/multimedia/progress-collision.htm Accessed on March 19, 2019.

Reichhardt, Tony, "The Spacewalk that Almost Killed Him," *Air and Space*, May 2014, www.airspacemag.com/space/spacewalk-almost-killed-him-180950135/?all Accessed on March 19, 2019.

"Spaceflight Mission Report, Voskhod 2," NASA, October 16, 2014, https://spaceflight.nasa.gov/outreach/SignificantIncidents/assets/spaceflight-mission-report_-voskhod-2.pdf Accessed on March 19, 2019.

Venogopal, Ramasamy, "Lost in Space: The First Space Walk," *Space Safety Magazine*, May 13, 2015, www.spacesafetymagazine.com/space-disasters/close-calls/lost-in-space-the-first-space-walk/ Accessed on March 19, 2019.

White, Mary, "Detailed Biographies of Apollo I Crew - Gus Grissom," NASA, August 4, 2006, https://history.nasa.gov/Apollo204/zorn/grissom.htm Accessed on March 19, 2019.

Woods, David, et al., "The Apollo 13 Flight Journal," NASA, May 14, 2016, https://history.nasa.gov/afj/ap13fj/index.html Accessed on March 19, 2019.

INDEX

ABOUT THE AUTHOR

Elizabeth Raum is the author of numerous books for young readers. She especially enjoys writing about people who face life-threatening challenges with courage and quick thinking. To learn more, visit her website at www.elizabethraumbooks.com.